Mileage Logbook

Name:	Position:
Adress:	
Mobile:	
Telephone:	
Email:	
Fax:	

Book info :

Book No.:	
Start Date:	End Date:

Notes:

____

____

____

____

____

____

Vehicle Mileage Logbook

Sheet no.:

Make :   Model :   Year :   License number :

DATE	PURPOSE OF TRAVEL	JOURNEY		ODOMETER READING			TOTAL MILES	
		From	To	Start	End	Distance (km)	Business	Private

Daily checks	Tires/ Wheel	Wipers	Lights	Mirrors	Horn	Seatbelts	Brakes	Coupling devices
Monday								
Tuesday								
Wednesday								
Thursday								
Friday								
Saturday								
Sunday								

Fuel Input				
Date	Quantity	Unit	Mileage	Units

Notes :

Signature :

Vehicle Mileage Logbook

Sheet no.:

Make :   Model :   Year :   License number :

DATE	PURPOSE OF TRAVEL	JOURNEY		ODOMETER READING			TOTAL MILES	
		From	To	Start	End	Distance (km)	Business	Private

Daily checks	Tires/ Wheel	Wipers	Lights	Mirrors	Horn	Seatbelts	Brakes	Coupling devices
Monday								
Tuesday								
Wednesday								
Thursday								
Friday								
Saturday								
Sunday								

Fuel Input				
Date	Quantity	Unit	Mileage	Units

Notes :

____

____

____

____

____

____

Signature :

Vehicle Mileage Logbook

Sheet no.:

Make :   Model :   Year :   License number :

DATE	PURPOSE OF TRAVEL	JOURNEY		ODOMETER READING			TOTAL MILES	
		From	To	Start	End	Distance (km)	Business	Private

Daily checks	Tires/Wheel	Wipers	Lights	Mirrors	Horn	Seatbelts	Brakes	Coupling devices
Monday								
Tuesday								
Wednesday								
Thursday								
Friday								
Saturday								
Sunday								

Fuel Input				
Date	Quantity	Unit	Mileage	Units

Notes :

Signature :

Vehicle Mileage Logbook

Sheet no.:	

Make :	Model :	Year :	License number :

DATE	PURPOSE OF TRAVEL	JOURNEY		ODOMETER READING			TOTAL MILES	
		From	To	Start	End	Distance (km)	Business	Private

Daily checks	Tires/ Wheel	Wipers	Lights	Mirrors	Horn	Seatbelts	Brakes	Coupling devices
Monday								
Tuesday								
Wednesday								
Thursday								
Friday								
Saturday								
Sunday								

Fuel Input				
Date	Quantity	Unit	Mileage	Units

Notes :
____
____
____
____
____
____

Signature :

Vehicle Mileage Logbook

Sheet no.:

Make :	Model :	Year :	License number :

DATE	PURPOSE OF TRAVEL	JOURNEY		ODOMETER READING			TOTAL MILES	
		From	To	Start	End	Distance (km)	Business	Private

Daily checks	Tires/Wheel	Wipers	Lights	Mirrors	Horn	Seatbelts	Brakes	Coupling devices
Monday								
Tuesday								
Wednesday								
Thursday								
Friday								
Saturday								
Sunday								

Fuel Input				
Date	Quantity	Unit	Mileage	Units

Notes :
____
____
____
____
____
____

Signature :

Vehicle Mileage Logbook

Sheet no.:

Make :   **Model :**   **Year :**   **License number :**

DATE	PURPOSE OF TRAVEL	JOURNEY		ODOMETER READING			TOTAL MILES	
		From	To	Start	End	Distance (km)	Business	Private

Daily checks	Tires/ Wheel	Wipers	Lights	Mirrors	Horn	Seatbelts	Brakes	Coupling devices
Monday								
Tuesday								
Wednesday								
Thursday								
Friday								
Saturday								
Sunday								

Fuel Input				
Date	Quantity	Unit	Mileage	Units

Notes :

____

____

____

____

____

____

Signature :

Vehicle Mileage Logbook

Sheet no.:

Make :   Model :   Year :   License number :

DATE	PURPOSE OF TRAVEL	JOURNEY		ODOMETER READING			TOTAL MILES	
		From	To	Start	End	Distance (km)	Business	Private

Daily checks	Tires/Wheel	Wipers	Lights	Mirrors	Horn	Seatbelts	Brakes	Coupling devices
Monday								
Tuesday								
Wednesday								
Thursday								
Friday								
Saturday								
Sunday								

Fuel Input				
Date	Quantity	Unit	Mileage	Units

Notes :

Signature :

Vehicle Mileage Logbook

Sheet no.:

Make : Model : Year : License number :

DATE	PURPOSE OF TRAVEL	JOURNEY		ODOMETER READING			TOTAL MILES	
		From	To	Start	End	Distance (km)	Business	Private

Daily checks	Tires/ Wheel	Wipers	Lights	Mirrors	Horn	Seatbelts	Brakes	Coupling devices
Monday								
Tuesday								
Wednesday								
Thursday								
Friday								
Saturday								
Sunday								

Fuel Input				
Date	Quantity	Unit	Mileage	Units

Notes :

Signature :

Vehicle Mileage Logbook

Sheet no.:

Make : **Model :** **Year :** **License number :**

DATE	PURPOSE OF TRAVEL	JOURNEY		ODOMETER READING			TOTAL MILES	
		From	To	Start	End	Distance (km)	Business	Private

Daily checks	Tires/Wheel	Wipers	Lights	Mirrors	Horn	Seatbelts	Brakes	Coupling devices
Monday								
Tuesday								
Wednesday								
Thursday								
Friday								
Saturday								
Sunday								

Fuel Input				
Date	Quantity	Unit	Mileage	Units

Notes :

____
____
____
____
____
____

Signature :

Vehicle Mileage Logbook

Make :   Model :   Year :   License number :

DATE	PURPOSE OF TRAVEL	JOURNEY		ODOMETER READING			TOTAL MILES	
		From	To	Start	End	Distance (km)	Business	Private

Daily checks	Tires/ Wheel	Wipers	Lights	Mirrors	Horn	Seatbelts	Brakes	Coupling devices
Monday								
Tuesday								
Wednesday								
Thursday								
Friday								
Saturday								
Sunday								

Fuel Input				
Date	Quantity	Unit	Mileage	Units

Notes :

____

____

____

____

____

____

Signature :

Vehicle Mileage Logbook

Sheet no.:

Make :	Model :	Year :	License number :

DATE	PURPOSE OF TRAVEL	JOURNEY		ODOMETER READING			TOTAL MILES	
		From	To	Start	End	Distance (km)	Business	Private

Daily checks	Tires/ Wheel	Wipers	Lights	Mirrors	Horn	Seatbelts	Brakes	Coupling devices
Monday								
Tuesday								
Wednesday								
Thursday								
Friday								
Saturday								
Sunday								

Fuel Input				
Date	Quantity	Unit	Mileage	Units

Notes :

____

____

____

____

____

____

____

Signature :

Vehicle Mileage Logbook

Sheet no.:

Make :   Model :   Year :   License number :

DATE	PURPOSE OF TRAVEL	JOURNEY		ODOMETER READING			TOTAL MILES	
		From	To	Start	End	Distance (km)	Business	Private

Daily checks	Tires/ Wheel	Wipers	Lights	Mirrors	Horn	Seatbelts	Brakes	Coupling devices
Monday								
Tuesday								
Wednesday								
Thursday								
Friday								
Saturday								
Sunday								

Fuel Input				
Date	Quantity	Unit	Mileage	Units

Notes :

____
____
____
____
____
____

Signature :

Vehicle Mileage Logbook

Sheet no.:

Make : **Model :** **Year :** **License number :**

DATE	PURPOSE OF TRAVEL	JOURNEY		ODOMETER READING			TOTAL MILES	
		From	To	Start	End	Distance (km)	Business	Private

Daily checks	Tires/ Wheel	Wipers	Lights	Mirrors	Horn	Seatbelts	Brakes	Coupling devices
Monday								
Tuesday								
Wednesday								
Thursday								
Friday								
Saturday								
Sunday								

Fuel Input				
Date	Quantity	Unit	Mileage	Units

Notes :

Signature :

Vehicle Mileage Logbook

Sheet no.:

Make : Model : Year : License number :

DATE	PURPOSE OF TRAVEL	JOURNEY		ODOMETER READING			TOTAL MILES	
		From	To	Start	End	Distance (km)	Business	Private

Daily checks	Tires/ Wheel	Wipers	Lights	Mirrors	Horn	Seatbelts	Brakes	Coupling devices
Monday								
Tuesday								
Wednesday								
Thursday								
Friday								
Saturday								
Sunday								

Fuel Input				
Date	Quantity	Unit	Mileage	Units

Notes :

____

____

____

____

____

____

____

Signature :

Vehicle Mileage Logbook

Sheet no.:

Make :   Model :   Year :   License number :

DATE	PURPOSE OF TRAVEL	JOURNEY		ODOMETER READING			TOTAL MILES	
		From	To	Start	End	Distance (km)	Business	Private

Daily checks	Tires/ Wheel	Wipers	Lights	Mirrors	Horn	Seatbelts	Brakes	Coupling devices
Monday								
Tuesday								
Wednesday								
Thursday								
Friday								
Saturday								
Sunday								

Fuel Input				
Date	Quantity	Unit	Mileage	Units

Notes :

____

Signature :

Vehicle Mileage Logbook

Sheet no.:

Make :   **Model :**   **Year :**   **License number :**

DATE	PURPOSE OF TRAVEL	JOURNEY		ODOMETER READING			TOTAL MILES	
		From	To	Start	End	Distance (km)	Business	Private

Daily checks	Tires/ Wheel	Wipers	Lights	Mirrors	Horn	Seatbelts	Brakes	Coupling devices
Monday								
Tuesday								
Wednesday								
Thursday								
Friday								
Saturday								
Sunday								

Fuel Input				
Date	Quantity	Unit	Mileage	Units

Notes :

Signature :

Vehicle Mileage Logbook

Sheet no.:

Make :   Model :   Year :   License number :

DATE	PURPOSE OF TRAVEL	JOURNEY		ODOMETER READING			TOTAL MILES	
		From	To	Start	End	Distance (km)	Business	Private

Daily checks	Tires/ Wheel	Wipers	Lights	Mirrors	Horn	Seatbelts	Brakes	Coupling devices
Monday								
Tuesday								
Wednesday								
Thursday								
Friday								
Saturday								
Sunday								

Fuel Input

Date	Quantity	Unit	Mileage	Units

Notes :

Signature :

Vehicle Mileage Logbook

Sheet no.:

Make :   Model :   Year :   License number :

DATE	PURPOSE OF TRAVEL	JOURNEY		ODOMETER READING			TOTAL MILES	
		From	To	Start	End	Distance (km)	Business	Private

Daily checks	Tires/ Wheel	Wipers	Lights	Mirrors	Horn	Seatbelts	Brakes	Coupling devices
Monday								
Tuesday								
Wednesday								
Thursday								
Friday								
Saturday								
Sunday								

Fuel Input				
Date	Quantity	Unit	Mileage	Units

Notes :
____
____
____
____
____
____

Signature :

Vehicle Mileage Logbook

Sheet no.:

Make : Model : Year : License number :

DATE	PURPOSE OF TRAVEL	JOURNEY		ODOMETER READING			TOTAL MILES	
		From	To	Start	End	Distance (km)	Business	Private

Daily checks	Tires/ Wheel	Wipers	Lights	Mirrors	Horn	Seatbelts	Brakes	Coupling devices
Monday								
Tuesday								
Wednesday								
Thursday								
Friday								
Saturday								
Sunday								

Fuel Input				
Date	Quantity	Unit	Mileage	Units

Notes :

Signature :

Vehicle Mileage Logbook

Sheet no.:

Make :   Model :   Year :   License number :

DATE	PURPOSE OF TRAVEL	JOURNEY		ODOMETER READING			TOTAL MILES	
		From	To	Start	End	Distance (km)	Business	Private

Daily checks	Tires/ Wheel	Wipers	Lights	Mirrors	Horn	Seatbelts	Brakes	Coupling devices
Monday								
Tuesday								
Wednesday								
Thursday								
Friday								
Saturday								
Sunday								

Fuel Input				
Date	Quantity	Unit	Mileage	Units

Notes :

Signature :

Vehicle Mileage Logbook

Make :	Model :	Year :	License number :	Sheet no.:

DATE	PURPOSE OF TRAVEL	JOURNEY		ODOMETER READING			TOTAL MILES	
		From	To	Start	End	Distance (km)	Business	Private

Daily checks	Tires/ Wheel	Wipers	Lights	Mirrors	Horn	Seatbelts	Brakes	Coupling devices
Monday								
Tuesday								
Wednesday								
Thursday								
Friday								
Saturday								
Sunday								

Fuel Input				
Date	Quantity	Unit	Mileage	Units

Notes :

Signature :

Vehicle Mileage Logbook

Sheet no.:

Make :   Model :   Year :   License number :

DATE	PURPOSE OF TRAVEL	JOURNEY		ODOMETER READING			TOTAL MILES	
		From	To	Start	End	Distance (km)	Business	Private

Daily checks	Tires/ Wheel	Wipers	Lights	Mirrors	Horn	Seatbelts	Brakes	Coupling devices
Monday								
Tuesday								
Wednesday								
Thursday								
Friday								
Saturday								
Sunday								

Fuel Input				
Date	Quantity	Unit	Mileage	Units

Notes :

Signature :

Vehicle Mileage Logbook

Sheet no.:

Make :　　Model :　　Year :　　License number :

DATE	PURPOSE OF TRAVEL	JOURNEY		ODOMETER READING			TOTAL MILES	
		From	To	Start	End	Distance (km)	Business	Private

Daily checks	Tires/ Wheel	Wipers	Lights	Mirrors	Horn	Seatbelts	Brakes	Coupling devices
Monday								
Tuesday								
Wednesday								
Thursday								
Friday								
Saturday								
Sunday								

Fuel Input				
Date	Quantity	Unit	Mileage	Units

Notes :

____
____
____
____
____
____

Signature :

Vehicle Mileage Logbook

Sheet no.:

Make :   Model :   Year :   License number :

DATE	PURPOSE OF TRAVEL	JOURNEY		ODOMETER READING			TOTAL MILES	
		From	To	Start	End	Distance (km)	Business	Private

Daily checks	Tires/ Wheel	Wipers	Lights	Mirrors	Horn	Seatbelts	Brakes	Coupling devices
Monday								
Tuesday								
Wednesday								
Thursday								
Friday								
Saturday								
Sunday								

Fuel Input				
Date	Quantity	Unit	Mileage	Units

Notes :

____

____

____

____

____

____

Signature :

Vehicle Mileage Logbook

Sheet no.:

Make :   Model :   Year :   License number :

DATE	PURPOSE OF TRAVEL	JOURNEY		ODOMETER READING			TOTAL MILES	
		From	To	Start	End	Distance (km)	Business	Private

Daily checks	Tires/ Wheel	Wipers	Lights	Mirrors	Horn	Seatbelts	Brakes	Coupling devices
Monday								
Tuesday								
Wednesday								
Thursday								
Friday								
Saturday								
Sunday								

Fuel Input				
Date	Quantity	Unit	Mileage	Units

Notes :

____

____

____

____

____

____

Signature :

Vehicle Mileage Logbook

Sheet no.:

Make :   Model :   Year :   License number :

DATE	PURPOSE OF TRAVEL	JOURNEY		ODOMETER READING			TOTAL MILES	
		From	To	Start	End	Distance (km)	Business	Private

Daily checks	Tires/ Wheel	Wipers	Lights	Mirrors	Horn	Seatbelts	Brakes	Coupling devices
Monday								
Tuesday								
Wednesday								
Thursday								
Friday								
Saturday								
Sunday								

Fuel Input				
Date	Quantity	Unit	Mileage	Units

Notes :

Signature :

Vehicle Mileage Logbook

Sheet no.:

Make :   Model :   Year :   License number :

DATE	PURPOSE OF TRAVEL	JOURNEY		ODOMETER READING			TOTAL MILES	
		From	To	Start	End	Distance (km)	Business	Private

Daily checks	Tires/ Wheel	Wipers	Lights	Mirrors	Horn	Seatbelts	Brakes	Coupling devices
Monday								
Tuesday								
Wednesday								
Thursday								
Friday								
Saturday								
Sunday								

Fuel Input				
Date	Quantity	Unit	Mileage	Units

Notes :

Signature :

Vehicle Mileage Logbook

Sheet no.:

Make :	Model :	Year :	License number :

DATE	PURPOSE OF TRAVEL	JOURNEY		ODOMETER READING			TOTAL MILES	
		From	To	Start	End	Distance (km)	Business	Private

Daily checks	Tires/ Wheel	Wipers	Lights	Mirrors	Horn	Seatbelts	Brakes	Coupling devices
Monday								
Tuesday								
Wednesday								
Thursday								
Friday								
Saturday								
Sunday								

Fuel Input				
Date	Quantity	Unit	Mileage	Units

Notes :

____

____

____

____

____

____

Signature :

Vehicle Mileage Logbook

Sheet no.:

Make :   Model :   Year :   License number :

DATE	PURPOSE OF TRAVEL	JOURNEY		ODOMETER READING			TOTAL MILES	
		From	To	Start	End	Distance (km)	Business	Private

Daily checks	Tires/ Wheel	Wipers	Lights	Mirrors	Horn	Seatbelts	Brakes	Coupling devices
Monday								
Tuesday								
Wednesday								
Thursday								
Friday								
Saturday								
Sunday								

Fuel Input				
Date	Quantity	Unit	Mileage	Units

Notes :

____

____

____

____

____

Signature :

Vehicle Mileage Logbook

Sheet no.:

Make :   Model :   Year :   License number :

DATE	PURPOSE OF TRAVEL	JOURNEY		ODOMETER READING			TOTAL MILES	
		From	To	Start	End	Distance (km)	Business	Private

Daily checks	Tires/ Wheel	Wipers	Lights	Mirrors	Horn	Seatbelts	Brakes	Coupling devices
Monday								
Tuesday								
Wednesday								
Thursday								
Friday								
Saturday								
Sunday								

Fuel Input				
Date	Quantity	Unit	Mileage	Units

Notes :

____
____
____
____
____
____

Signature :

Vehicle Mileage Logbook

Sheet no.:

Make :   Model :   Year :   License number :

DATE	PURPOSE OF TRAVEL	JOURNEY		ODOMETER READING			TOTAL MILES	
		From	To	Start	End	Distance (km)	Business	Private

Daily checks	Tires/ Wheel	Wipers	Lights	Mirrors	Horn	Seatbelts	Brakes	Coupling devices
Monday								
Tuesday								
Wednesday								
Thursday								
Friday								
Saturday								
Sunday								

Fuel Input				
Date	Quantity	Unit	Mileage	Units

Notes :

Signature :

Vehicle Mileage Logbook

	Sheet no.:

Make :	Model :	Year :	License number :

DATE	PURPOSE OF TRAVEL	JOURNEY		ODOMETER READING			TOTAL MILES	
		From	To	Start	End	Distance (km)	Business	Private

Daily checks	Tires/ Wheel	Wipers	Lights	Mirrors	Horn	Seatbelts	Brakes	Coupling devices
Monday								
Tuesday								
Wednesday								
Thursday								
Friday								
Saturday								
Sunday								

Fuel Input				
Date	Quantity	Unit	Mileage	Units

Notes :

____
____
____
____
____
____

Signature :

Vehicle Mileage Logbook

Sheet no.:

Make :	Model :	Year :	License number :

DATE	PURPOSE OF TRAVEL	JOURNEY		ODOMETER READING			TOTAL MILES	
		From	To	Start	End	Distance (km)	Business	Private

Daily checks	Tires/ Wheel	Wipers	Lights	Mirrors	Horn	Seatbelts	Brakes	Coupling devices
Monday								
Tuesday								
Wednesday								
Thursday								
Friday								
Saturday								
Sunday								

Fuel Input				
Date	Quantity	Unit	Mileage	Units

Notes :

____

____

____

____

____

____

Signature :

Vehicle Mileage Logbook

Sheet no.:

Make : | **Model :** | **Year :** | **License number :**

DATE	PURPOSE OF TRAVEL	JOURNEY		ODOMETER READING			TOTAL MILES	
		From	To	Start	End	Distance (km)	Business	Private

Daily checks	Tires/ Wheel	Wipers	Lights	Mirrors	Horn	Seatbelts	Brakes	Coupling devices
Monday								
Tuesday								
Wednesday								
Thursday								
Friday								
Saturday								
Sunday								

Fuel Input				
Date	Quantity	Unit	Mileage	Units

Notes :

____

____

____

____

____

____

Signature :

Vehicle Mileage Logbook

Sheet no.:

Make :   Model :   Year :   License number :

DATE	PURPOSE OF TRAVEL	JOURNEY		ODOMETER READING			TOTAL MILES	
		From	To	Start	End	Distance (km)	Business	Private

Daily checks	Tires/ Wheel	Wipers	Lights	Mirrors	Horn	Seatbelts	Brakes	Coupling devices
Monday								
Tuesday								
Wednesday								
Thursday								
Friday								
Saturday								
Sunday								

Fuel Input				
Date	Quantity	Unit	Mileage	Units

Notes :

Signature :

Vehicle Mileage Logbook

Sheet no.:

Make :   Model :   Year :   License number :

DATE	PURPOSE OF TRAVEL	JOURNEY		ODOMETER READING			TOTAL MILES	
		From	To	Start	End	Distance (km)	Business	Private

Daily checks	Tires/ Wheel	Wipers	Lights	Mirrors	Horn	Seatbelts	Brakes	Coupling devices
Monday								
Tuesday								
Wednesday								
Thursday								
Friday								
Saturday								
Sunday								

Fuel Input				
Date	Quantity	Unit	Mileage	Units

Notes :

____

____

____

____

____

____

Signature :

Vehicle Mileage Logbook

Sheet no.:

Make :   Model :   Year :   License number :

DATE	PURPOSE OF TRAVEL	JOURNEY		ODOMETER READING			TOTAL MILES	
		From	To	Start	End	Distance (km)	Business	Private

Daily checks	Tires/ Wheel	Wipers	Lights	Mirrors	Horn	Seatbelts	Brakes	Coupling devices
Monday								
Tuesday								
Wednesday								
Thursday								
Friday								
Saturday								
Sunday								

Fuel Input				
Date	Quantity	Unit	Mileage	Units

Notes :

Signature :

Vehicle Mileage Logbook

Sheet no.:

Make :   Model :   Year :   License number :

DATE	PURPOSE OF TRAVEL	JOURNEY		ODOMETER READING			TOTAL MILES	
		From	To	Start	End	Distance (km)	Business	Private

Daily checks	Tires/ Wheel	Wipers	Lights	Mirrors	Horn	Seatbelts	Brakes	Coupling devices
Monday								
Tuesday								
Wednesday								
Thursday								
Friday								
Saturday								
Sunday								

Fuel Input				
Date	Quantity	Unit	Mileage	Units

Notes :

____

____

____

____

____

____

Signature :

Vehicle Mileage Logbook

Sheet no.:

Make : | Model : | Year : | License number :

DATE	PURPOSE OF TRAVEL	JOURNEY		ODOMETER READING			TOTAL MILES	
		From	To	Start	End	Distance (km)	Business	Private

Daily checks	Tires/ Wheel	Wipers	Lights	Mirrors	Horn	Seatbelts	Brakes	Coupling devices
Monday								
Tuesday								
Wednesday								
Thursday								
Friday								
Saturday								
Sunday								

Fuel Input				
Date	Quantity	Unit	Mileage	Units

Notes :

Signature :

Vehicle Mileage Logbook

Sheet no.:

Make :   Model :   Year :   License number :

DATE	PURPOSE OF TRAVEL	JOURNEY		ODOMETER READING			TOTAL MILES	
		From	To	Start	End	Distance (km)	Business	Private

Daily checks	Tires/ Wheel	Wipers	Lights	Mirrors	Horn	Seatbelts	Brakes	Coupling devices
Monday								
Tuesday								
Wednesday								
Thursday								
Friday								
Saturday								
Sunday								

Fuel Input				
Date	Quantity	Unit	Mileage	Units

Notes :

____

____

____

____

____

____

Signature :

Vehicle Mileage Logbook

Sheet no.:

Make :   Model :   Year :   License number :

DATE	PURPOSE OF TRAVEL	JOURNEY		ODOMETER READING			TOTAL MILES	
		From	To	Start	End	Distance (km)	Business	Private

Daily checks	Tires/ Wheel	Wipers	Lights	Mirrors	Horn	Seatbelts	Brakes	Coupling devices
Monday								
Tuesday								
Wednesday								
Thursday								
Friday								
Saturday								
Sunday								

Fuel Input				
Date	Quantity	Unit	Mileage	Units

Notes :

Signature :

Vehicle Mileage Logbook

Sheet no.:

Make :	Model :	Year :	License number :

DATE	PURPOSE OF TRAVEL	JOURNEY		ODOMETER READING			TOTAL MILES	
		From	To	Start	End	Distance (km)	Business	Private

Daily checks	Tires/ Wheel	Wipers	Lights	Mirrors	Horn	Seatbelts	Brakes	Coupling devices
Monday								
Tuesday								
Wednesday								
Thursday								
Friday								
Saturday								
Sunday								

Fuel Input				
Date	Quantity	Unit	Mileage	Units

Notes :

____

____

____

____

____

Signature :

Vehicle Mileage Logbook

Sheet no.:

Make :   Model :   Year :   License number :

DATE	PURPOSE OF TRAVEL	JOURNEY		ODOMETER READING			TOTAL MILES	
		From	To	Start	End	Distance (km)	Business	Private

Daily checks	Tires/ Wheel	Wipers	Lights	Mirrors	Horn	Seatbelts	Brakes	Coupling devices
Monday								
Tuesday								
Wednesday								
Thursday								
Friday								
Saturday								
Sunday								

Fuel Input				
Date	Quantity	Unit	Mileage	Units

Notes :

Signature :

Vehicle Mileage Logbook

Sheet no.:

Make :   Model :   Year :   License number :

DATE	PURPOSE OF TRAVEL	JOURNEY		ODOMETER READING			TOTAL MILES	
		From	To	Start	End	Distance (km)	Business	Private

Daily checks	Tires/ Wheel	Wipers	Lights	Mirrors	Horn	Seatbelts	Brakes	Coupling devices
Monday								
Tuesday								
Wednesday								
Thursday								
Friday								
Saturday								
Sunday								

Fuel Input				
Date	Quantity	Unit	Mileage	Units

Notes :

____

____

____

____

____

____

Signature :

Vehicle Mileage Logbook

Sheet no.:

Make :   Model :   Year :   License number :

DATE	PURPOSE OF TRAVEL	JOURNEY		ODOMETER READING			TOTAL MILES	
		From	To	Start	End	Distance (km)	Business	Private

Daily checks	Tires/ Wheel	Wipers	Lights	Mirrors	Horn	Seatbelts	Brakes	Coupling devices
Monday								
Tuesday								
Wednesday								
Thursday								
Friday								
Saturday								
Sunday								

Fuel Input

Date	Quantity	Unit	Mileage	Units

Notes :

Signature :

Vehicle Mileage Logbook

Sheet no.:

Make :   Model :   Year :   License number :

DATE	PURPOSE OF TRAVEL	JOURNEY		ODOMETER READING			TOTAL MILES	
		From	To	Start	End	Distance (km)	Business	Private

Daily checks	Tires/ Wheel	Wipers	Lights	Mirrors	Horn	Seatbelts	Brakes	Coupling devices
Monday								
Tuesday								
Wednesday								
Thursday								
Friday								
Saturday								
Sunday								

Fuel Input				
Date	Quantity	Unit	Mileage	Units

Notes :

____

____

____

____

____

Signature :

Vehicle Mileage Logbook

Sheet no.:

Make :   Model :   Year :   License number :

DATE	PURPOSE OF TRAVEL	JOURNEY		ODOMETER READING			TOTAL MILES	
		From	To	Start	End	Distance (km)	Business	Private

Daily checks	Tires/ Wheel	Wipers	Lights	Mirrors	Horn	Seatbelts	Brakes	Coupling devices
Monday								
Tuesday								
Wednesday								
Thursday								
Friday								
Saturday								
Sunday								

Fuel Input				
Date	Quantity	Unit	Mileage	Units

Notes :

Signature :

Vehicle Mileage Logbook

Sheet no.:

Make : Model : Year : License number :

DATE	PURPOSE OF TRAVEL	JOURNEY		ODOMETER READING			TOTAL MILES	
		From	To	Start	End	Distance (km)	Business	Private

Daily checks	Tires/ Wheel	Wipers	Lights	Mirrors	Horn	Seatbelts	Brakes	Coupling devices
Monday								
Tuesday								
Wednesday								
Thursday								
Friday								
Saturday								
Sunday								

Fuel Input				
Date	Quantity	Unit	Mileage	Units

Notes :

Signature :

Vehicle Mileage Logbook

Sheet no.:

Make :   Model :   Year :   License number :

DATE	PURPOSE OF TRAVEL	JOURNEY		ODOMETER READING			TOTAL MILES	
		From	To	Start	End	Distance (km)	Business	Private

Daily checks	Tires/ Wheel	Wipers	Lights	Mirrors	Horn	Seatbelts	Brakes	Coupling devices
Monday								
Tuesday								
Wednesday								
Thursday								
Friday								
Saturday								
Sunday								

Fuel Input				
Date	Quantity	Unit	Mileage	Units

Notes :

____
____
____
____
____
____

Signature :

Vehicle Mileage Logbook

	Sheet no.:

Make :	Model :	Year :	License number :

DATE	PURPOSE OF TRAVEL	JOURNEY		ODOMETER READING			TOTAL MILES	
		From	To	Start	End	Distance (km)	Business	Private

Daily checks	Tires/Wheel	Wipers	Lights	Mirrors	Horn	Seatbelts	Brakes	Coupling devices
Monday								
Tuesday								
Wednesday								
Thursday								
Friday								
Saturday								
Sunday								

Fuel Input				
Date	Quantity	Unit	Mileage	Units

Notes :

____

____

____

____

____

____

____

Signature :

Vehicle Mileage Logbook

Sheet no.:

Make :   Model :   Year :   License number :

DATE	PURPOSE OF TRAVEL	JOURNEY		ODOMETER READING			TOTAL MILES	
		From	To	Start	End	Distance (km)	Business	Private

Daily checks	Tires/ Wheel	Wipers	Lights	Mirrors	Horn	Seatbelts	Brakes	Coupling devices
Monday								
Tuesday								
Wednesday								
Thursday								
Friday								
Saturday								
Sunday								

Fuel Input				
Date	Quantity	Unit	Mileage	Units

Notes :

____

____

____

____

____

____

____

Signature :

Vehicle Mileage Logbook

Sheet no.:

Make :	Model :	Year :	License number :

DATE	PURPOSE OF TRAVEL	JOURNEY		ODOMETER READING			TOTAL MILES	
		From	To	Start	End	Distance (km)	Business	Private

Daily checks	Tires/ Wheel	Wipers	Lights	Mirrors	Horn	Seatbelts	Brakes	Coupling devices
Monday								
Tuesday								
Wednesday								
Thursday								
Friday								
Saturday								
Sunday								

Fuel Input				
Date	Quantity	Unit	Mileage	Units

Notes :

____

____

____

____

____

____

Signature :

Vehicle Mileage Logbook

Sheet no.:

Make :	Model :	Year :	License number :

DATE	PURPOSE OF TRAVEL	JOURNEY		ODOMETER READING			TOTAL MILES	
		From	To	Start	End	Distance (km)	Business	Private

Daily checks	Tires/ Wheel	Wipers	Lights	Mirrors	Horn	Seatbelts	Brakes	Coupling devices
Monday								
Tuesday								
Wednesday								
Thursday								
Friday								
Saturday								
Sunday								

Fuel Input				
Date	Quantity	Unit	Mileage	Units

Notes :

Signature :

Vehicle Mileage Logbook

Sheet no.:

Make : | **Model :** | **Year :** | **License number :**

DATE	PURPOSE OF TRAVEL	JOURNEY		ODOMETER READING			TOTAL MILES	
		From	To	Start	End	Distance (km)	Business	Private

Daily checks	Tires/Wheel	Wipers	Lights	Mirrors	Horn	Seatbelts	Brakes	Coupling devices
Monday								
Tuesday								
Wednesday								
Thursday								
Friday								
Saturday								
Sunday								

Fuel Input

Date	Quantity	Unit	Mileage	Units

Notes :

____

____

____

____

____

____

Signature :

Vehicle Mileage Logbook

Sheet no.:

Make :   Model :   Year :   License number :

DATE	PURPOSE OF TRAVEL	JOURNEY		ODOMETER READING			TOTAL MILES	
		From	To	Start	End	Distance (km)	Business	Private

Daily checks	Tires/ Wheel	Wipers	Lights	Mirrors	Horn	Seatbelts	Brakes	Coupling devices
Monday								
Tuesday								
Wednesday								
Thursday								
Friday								
Saturday								
Sunday								

Fuel Input				
Date	Quantity	Unit	Mileage	Units

Notes :

____

____

____

____

____

____

Signature :

Vehicle Mileage Logbook

Sheet no.:

Make :   Model :   Year :   License number :

DATE	PURPOSE OF TRAVEL	JOURNEY		ODOMETER READING			TOTAL MILES	
		From	To	Start	End	Distance (km)	Business	Private

Daily checks	Tires/ Wheel	Wipers	Lights	Mirrors	Horn	Seatbelts	Brakes	Coupling devices
Monday								
Tuesday								
Wednesday								
Thursday								
Friday								
Saturday								
Sunday								

Fuel Input				
Date	Quantity	Unit	Mileage	Units

Notes :

____

____

____

____

____

____

____

Signature :

Vehicle Mileage Logbook

Sheet no.:

Make :   Model :   Year :   License number :

DATE	PURPOSE OF TRAVEL	JOURNEY		ODOMETER READING			TOTAL MILES	
		From	To	Start	End	Distance (km)	Business	Private

Daily checks	Tires/ Wheel	Wipers	Lights	Mirrors	Horn	Seatbelts	Brakes	Coupling devices
Monday								
Tuesday								
Wednesday								
Thursday								
Friday								
Saturday								
Sunday								

Fuel Input				
Date	Quantity	Unit	Mileage	Units

Notes :
____
____
____
____
____
____

Signature :

Vehicle Mileage Logbook

Make :   Model :   Year :   License number :

DATE	PURPOSE OF TRAVEL	JOURNEY		ODOMETER READING			TOTAL MILES	
		From	To	Start	End	Distance (km)	Business	Private

Daily checks	Tires/ Wheel	Wipers	Lights	Mirrors	Horn	Seatbelts	Brakes	Coupling devices
Monday								
Tuesday								
Wednesday								
Thursday								
Friday								
Saturday								
Sunday								

Fuel Input				
Date	Quantity	Unit	Mileage	Units

Notes :

____

____

____

____

____

____

Signature :

Vehicle Mileage Logbook

Sheet no.:

Make :   Model :   Year :   License number :

DATE	PURPOSE OF TRAVEL	JOURNEY		ODOMETER READING			TOTAL MILES	
		From	To	Start	End	Distance (km)	Business	Private

Daily checks	Tires/ Wheel	Wipers	Lights	Mirrors	Horn	Seatbelts	Brakes	Coupling devices
Monday								
Tuesday								
Wednesday								
Thursday								
Friday								
Saturday								
Sunday								

Fuel Input				
Date	Quantity	Unit	Mileage	Units

Notes :

Signature :

Vehicle Mileage Logbook

Sheet no.:

Make :   Model :   Year :   License number :

DATE	PURPOSE OF TRAVEL	JOURNEY		ODOMETER READING			TOTAL MILES	
		From	To	Start	End	Distance (km)	Business	Private

Daily checks	Tires/ Wheel	Wipers	Lights	Mirrors	Horn	Seatbelts	Brakes	Coupling devices
Monday								
Tuesday								
Wednesday								
Thursday								
Friday								
Saturday								
Sunday								

Fuel Input				
Date	Quantity	Unit	Mileage	Units

Notes :

____

____

____

____

____

Signature :

Vehicle Mileage Logbook

			Sheet no.:
Make :	Model :	Year :	License number :

DATE	PURPOSE OF TRAVEL	JOURNEY		ODOMETER READING			TOTAL MILES	
		From	To	Start	End	Distance (km)	Business	Private

Daily checks	Tires/ Wheel	Wipers	Lights	Mirrors	Horn	Seatbelts	Brakes	Coupling devices
Monday								
Tuesday								
Wednesday								
Thursday								
Friday								
Saturday								
Sunday								

Fuel Input				
Date	Quantity	Unit	Mileage	Units

Notes :

____

____

____

____

____

____

Signature :

Vehicle Mileage Logbook

Sheet no.:

Make :　　Model :　　Year :　　License number :

DATE	PURPOSE OF TRAVEL	JOURNEY		ODOMETER READING			TOTAL MILES	
		From	To	Start	End	Distance (km)	Business	Private

Daily checks	Tires/ Wheel	Wipers	Lights	Mirrors	Horn	Seatbelts	Brakes	Coupling devices
Monday								
Tuesday								
Wednesday								
Thursday								
Friday								
Saturday								
Sunday								

Fuel Input

Date	Quantity	Unit	Mileage	Units

Notes :

____
____
____
____
____
____

Signature :

Vehicle Mileage Logbook

Sheet no.:

Make :   Model :   Year :   License number :

DATE	PURPOSE OF TRAVEL	JOURNEY		ODOMETER READING			TOTAL MILES	
		From	To	Start	End	Distance (km)	Business	Private

Daily checks	Tires/ Wheel	Wipers	Lights	Mirrors	Horn	Seatbelts	Brakes	Coupling devices
Monday								
Tuesday								
Wednesday								
Thursday								
Friday								
Saturday								
Sunday								

Fuel Input				
Date	Quantity	Unit	Mileage	Units

Notes :

____

____

____

____

____

____

Signature :

Vehicle Mileage Logbook

Sheet no.:

Make : Model : Year : License number :

DATE	PURPOSE OF TRAVEL	JOURNEY		ODOMETER READING			TOTAL MILES	
		From	To	Start	End	Distance (km)	Business	Private

Daily checks	Tires/ Wheel	Wipers	Lights	Mirrors	Horn	Seatbelts	Brakes	Coupling devices
Monday								
Tuesday								
Wednesday								
Thursday								
Friday								
Saturday								
Sunday								

Fuel Input				
Date	Quantity	Unit	Mileage	Units

Notes :

____

____

____

____

____

____

Signature :

Vehicle Mileage Logbook

Sheet no.:

Make :   Model :   Year :   License number :

DATE	PURPOSE OF TRAVEL	JOURNEY		ODOMETER READING			TOTAL MILES	
		From	To	Start	End	Distance (km)	Business	Private

Daily checks	Tires/ Wheel	Wipers	Lights	Mirrors	Horn	Seatbelts	Brakes	Coupling devices
Monday								
Tuesday								
Wednesday								
Thursday								
Friday								
Saturday								
Sunday								

Fuel Input				
Date	Quantity	Unit	Mileage	Units

Notes :

Signature :

Vehicle Mileage Logbook

Sheet no.:

Make :   Model :   Year :   License number :

DATE	PURPOSE OF TRAVEL	JOURNEY		ODOMETER READING			TOTAL MILES	
		From	To	Start	End	Distance (km)	Business	Private

Daily checks	Tires/Wheel	Wipers	Lights	Mirrors	Horn	Seatbelts	Brakes	Coupling devices
Monday								
Tuesday								
Wednesday								
Thursday								
Friday								
Saturday								
Sunday								

Fuel Input				
Date	Quantity	Unit	Mileage	Units

Notes :

____

____

____

____

____

____

Signature :

Vehicle Mileage Logbook

Sheet no.:

Make : Model : Year : License number :

DATE	PURPOSE OF TRAVEL	JOURNEY		ODOMETER READING			TOTAL MILES	
		From	To	Start	End	Distance (km)	Business	Private

Daily checks	Tires/ Wheel	Wipers	Lights	Mirrors	Horn	Seatbelts	Brakes	Coupling devices
Monday								
Tuesday								
Wednesday								
Thursday								
Friday								
Saturday								
Sunday								

Fuel Input				
Date	Quantity	Unit	Mileage	Units

Notes :

Signature :

Vehicle Mileage Logbook

Sheet no.:

Make :   Model :   Year :   License number :

DATE	PURPOSE OF TRAVEL	JOURNEY		ODOMETER READING			TOTAL MILES	
		From	To	Start	End	Distance (km)	Business	Private

Daily checks	Tires/ Wheel	Wipers	Lights	Mirrors	Horn	Seatbelts	Brakes	Coupling devices
Monday								
Tuesday								
Wednesday								
Thursday								
Friday								
Saturday								
Sunday								

Fuel Input				
Date	Quantity	Unit	Mileage	Units

Notes :

____

____

____

____

____

Signature :

Vehicle Mileage Logbook

Sheet no.:

Make :   Model :   Year :   License number :

DATE	PURPOSE OF TRAVEL	JOURNEY		ODOMETER READING			TOTAL MILES	
		From	To	Start	End	Distance (km)	Business	Private

Daily checks	Tires/ Wheel	Wipers	Lights	Mirrors	Horn	Seatbelts	Brakes	Coupling devices
Monday								
Tuesday								
Wednesday								
Thursday								
Friday								
Saturday								
Sunday								

Fuel Input				
Date	Quantity	Unit	Mileage	Units

Notes :

Signature :

Vehicle Mileage Logbook

Make :   Model :   Year :   License number :

DATE	PURPOSE OF TRAVEL	JOURNEY		ODOMETER READING			TOTAL MILES	
		From	To	Start	End	Distance (km)	Business	Private

Daily checks	Tires/ Wheel	Wipers	Lights	Mirrors	Horn	Seatbelts	Brakes	Coupling devices
Monday								
Tuesday								
Wednesday								
Thursday								
Friday								
Saturday								
Sunday								

Fuel Input				
Date	Quantity	Unit	Mileage	Units

Notes :

____

____

____

____

____

____

Signature :

Vehicle Mileage Logbook

Sheet no.:

Make : Model : Year : License number :

DATE	PURPOSE OF TRAVEL	JOURNEY		ODOMETER READING			TOTAL MILES	
		From	To	Start	End	Distance (km)	Business	Private

Daily checks	Tires/ Wheel	Wipers	Lights	Mirrors	Horn	Seatbelts	Brakes	Coupling devices
Monday								
Tuesday								
Wednesday								
Thursday								
Friday								
Saturday								
Sunday								

Fuel Input				
Date	Quantity	Unit	Mileage	Units

Notes :

Signature :

Vehicle Mileage Logbook

Sheet no.:

Make :   Model :   Year :   License number :

DATE	PURPOSE OF TRAVEL	JOURNEY		ODOMETER READING			TOTAL MILES	
		From	To	Start	End	Distance (km)	Business	Private

Daily checks	Tires/ Wheel	Wipers	Lights	Mirrors	Horn	Seatbelts	Brakes	Coupling devices
Monday								
Tuesday								
Wednesday								
Thursday								
Friday								
Saturday								
Sunday								

Fuel Input				
Date	Quantity	Unit	Mileage	Units

Notes :

Signature :

Vehicle Mileage Logbook

Sheet no.:

Make : **Model :** **Year :** **License number :**

DATE	PURPOSE OF TRAVEL	JOURNEY		ODOMETER READING			TOTAL MILES	
		From	To	Start	End	Distance (km)	Business	Private

Daily checks	Tires/ Wheel	Wipers	Lights	Mirrors	Horn	Seatbelts	Brakes	Coupling devices
Monday								
Tuesday								
Wednesday								
Thursday								
Friday								
Saturday								
Sunday								

Fuel Input

Date	Quantity	Unit	Mileage	Units

Notes :

Signature :

Vehicle Mileage Logbook

Sheet no.:

Make :   Model :   Year :   License number :

DATE	PURPOSE OF TRAVEL	JOURNEY		ODOMETER READING			TOTAL MILES	
		From	To	Start	End	Distance (km)	Business	Private

Daily checks	Tires/ Wheel	Wipers	Lights	Mirrors	Horn	Seatbelts	Brakes	Coupling devices
Monday								
Tuesday								
Wednesday								
Thursday								
Friday								
Saturday								
Sunday								

Fuel Input				
Date	Quantity	Unit	Mileage	Units

Notes :

____

____

____

____

____

____

Signature :

Vehicle Mileage Logbook

Sheet no.:

Make :   Model :   Year :   License number :

DATE	PURPOSE OF TRAVEL	JOURNEY		ODOMETER READING			TOTAL MILES	
		From	To	Start	End	Distance (km)	Business	Private

Daily checks	Tires/ Wheel	Wipers	Lights	Mirrors	Horn	Seatbelts	Brakes	Coupling devices
Monday								
Tuesday								
Wednesday								
Thursday								
Friday								
Saturday								
Sunday								

Fuel Input				
Date	Quantity	Unit	Mileage	Units

Notes :

Signature :

Vehicle Mileage Logbook

Sheet no.:

Make :	Model :	Year :	License number :

DATE	PURPOSE OF TRAVEL	JOURNEY		ODOMETER READING			TOTAL MILES	
		From	To	Start	End	Distance (km)	Business	Private

Daily checks	Tires/ Wheel	Wipers	Lights	Mirrors	Horn	Seatbelts	Brakes	Coupling devices
Monday								
Tuesday								
Wednesday								
Thursday								
Friday								
Saturday								
Sunday								

Fuel Input				
Date	Quantity	Unit	Mileage	Units

Notes :

Signature :

Vehicle Mileage Logbook

Sheet no.:

Make :   Model :   Year :   License number :

DATE	PURPOSE OF TRAVEL	JOURNEY		ODOMETER READING			TOTAL MILES	
		From	To	Start	End	Distance (km)	Business	Private

Daily checks	Tires/ Wheel	Wipers	Lights	Mirrors	Horn	Seatbelts	Brakes	Coupling devices
Monday								
Tuesday								
Wednesday								
Thursday								
Friday								
Saturday								
Sunday								

Fuel Input				
Date	Quantity	Unit	Mileage	Units

Notes :

____

Signature :

Vehicle Mileage Logbook

Sheet no.:

Make :   Model :   Year :   License number :

DATE	PURPOSE OF TRAVEL	JOURNEY		ODOMETER READING			TOTAL MILES	
		From	To	Start	End	Distance (km)	Business	Private

Daily checks	Tires/Wheel	Wipers	Lights	Mirrors	Horn	Seatbelts	Brakes	Coupling devices
Monday								
Tuesday								
Wednesday								
Thursday								
Friday								
Saturday								
Sunday								

Fuel Input				
Date	Quantity	Unit	Mileage	Units

Notes :

____

____

____

____

____

____

Signature :

Vehicle Mileage Logbook

Sheet no.:

Make : **Model :** **Year :** **License number :**

DATE	PURPOSE OF TRAVEL	JOURNEY		ODOMETER READING			TOTAL MILES	
		From	To	Start	End	Distance (km)	Business	Private

Daily checks	Tires/ Wheel	Wipers	Lights	Mirrors	Horn	Seatbelts	Brakes	Coupling devices
Monday								
Tuesday								
Wednesday								
Thursday								
Friday								
Saturday								
Sunday								

Fuel Input				
Date	Quantity	Unit	Mileage	Units

Notes :

Signature :

Vehicle Mileage Logbook

Sheet no.:

Make :   Model :   Year :   License number :

DATE	PURPOSE OF TRAVEL	JOURNEY		ODOMETER READING			TOTAL MILES	
		From	To	Start	End	Distance (km)	Business	Private

Daily checks	Tires/ Wheel	Wipers	Lights	Mirrors	Horn	Seatbelts	Brakes	Coupling devices
Monday								
Tuesday								
Wednesday								
Thursday								
Friday								
Saturday								
Sunday								

Fuel Input				
Date	Quantity	Unit	Mileage	Units

Notes :

____

____

____

____

____

____

Signature :

Vehicle Mileage Logbook

Sheet no.:

Make :	Model :	Year :	License number :

DATE	PURPOSE OF TRAVEL	JOURNEY		ODOMETER READING			TOTAL MILES	
		From	To	Start	End	Distance (km)	Business	Private

Daily checks	Tires/ Wheel	Wipers	Lights	Mirrors	Horn	Seatbelts	Brakes	Coupling devices
Monday								
Tuesday								
Wednesday								
Thursday								
Friday								
Saturday								
Sunday								

Fuel Input				
Date	Quantity	Unit	Mileage	Units

Notes :

____

____

____

____

____

____

Signature :

Vehicle Mileage Logbook

Sheet no.:

Make :   Model :   Year :   License number :

DATE	PURPOSE OF TRAVEL	JOURNEY		ODOMETER READING			TOTAL MILES	
		From	To	Start	End	Distance (km)	Business	Private

Daily checks	Tires/ Wheel	Wipers	Lights	Mirrors	Horn	Seatbelts	Brakes	Coupling devices
Monday								
Tuesday								
Wednesday								
Thursday								
Friday								
Saturday								
Sunday								

Fuel Input				
Date	Quantity	Unit	Mileage	Units

Notes :

Signature :

Vehicle Mileage Logbook

Sheet no.:

Make : | Model : | Year : | License number :

DATE	PURPOSE OF TRAVEL	JOURNEY		ODOMETER READING			TOTAL MILES	
		From	To	Start	End	Distance (km)	Business	Private

Daily checks	Tires/ Wheel	Wipers	Lights	Mirrors	Horn	Seatbelts	Brakes	Coupling devices
Monday								
Tuesday								
Wednesday								
Thursday								
Friday								
Saturday								
Sunday								

Fuel Input				
Date	Quantity	Unit	Mileage	Units

Notes :

Signature :

Vehicle Mileage Logbook

Sheet no.:

Make :	Model :	Year :	License number :

DATE	PURPOSE OF TRAVEL	JOURNEY		ODOMETER READING			TOTAL MILES	
		From	To	Start	End	Distance (km)	Business	Private

Daily checks	Tires/ Wheel	Wipers	Lights	Mirrors	Horn	Seatbelts	Brakes	Coupling devices
Monday								
Tuesday								
Wednesday								
Thursday								
Friday								
Saturday								
Sunday								

Fuel Input				
Date	Quantity	Unit	Mileage	Units

Notes :

____

Signature :

Vehicle Mileage Logbook

Sheet no.:

Make :   Model :   Year :   License number :

DATE	PURPOSE OF TRAVEL	JOURNEY		ODOMETER READING			TOTAL MILES	
		From	To	Start	End	Distance (km)	Business	Private

Daily checks	Tires/ Wheel	Wipers	Lights	Mirrors	Horn	Seatbelts	Brakes	Coupling devices
Monday								
Tuesday								
Wednesday								
Thursday								
Friday								
Saturday								
Sunday								

Fuel Input				
Date	Quantity	Unit	Mileage	Units

Notes :

____

Signature :

Vehicle Mileage Logbook

Sheet no.:

Make :   **Model :**   **Year :**   **License number :**

DATE	PURPOSE OF TRAVEL	JOURNEY		ODOMETER READING			TOTAL MILES	
		From	To	Start	End	Distance (km)	Business	Private

Daily checks	Tires/ Wheel	Wipers	Lights	Mirrors	Horn	Seatbelts	Brakes	Coupling devices
Monday								
Tuesday								
Wednesday								
Thursday								
Friday								
Saturday								
Sunday								

Fuel Input				
Date	Quantity	Unit	Mileage	Units

Notes :

Signature :

Vehicle Mileage Logbook

Sheet no.:

Make : | Model : | Year : | License number :

DATE	PURPOSE OF TRAVEL	JOURNEY		ODOMETER READING			TOTAL MILES	
		From	To	Start	End	Distance (km)	Business	Private

Daily checks	Tires/ Wheel	Wipers	Lights	Mirrors	Horn	Seatbelts	Brakes	Coupling devices
Monday								
Tuesday								
Wednesday								
Thursday								
Friday								
Saturday								
Sunday								

Fuel Input				
Date	Quantity	Unit	Mileage	Units

Notes :

Signature :

Vehicle Mileage Logbook

Sheet no.:

| Make : | | Model : | | Year : | | License number : |

DATE	PURPOSE OF TRAVEL	JOURNEY		ODOMETER READING			TOTAL MILES	
		From	To	Start	End	Distance (km)	Business	Private

Daily checks	Tires/ Wheel	Wipers	Lights	Mirrors	Horn	Seatbelts	Brakes	Coupling devices
Monday								
Tuesday								
Wednesday								
Thursday								
Friday								
Saturday								
Sunday								

Fuel Input				
Date	Quantity	Unit	Mileage	Units

Notes :

____

____

____

____

____

____

____

Signature :

Vehicle Mileage Logbook

Sheet no.:

Make :	Model :	Year :	License number :

DATE	PURPOSE OF TRAVEL	JOURNEY		ODOMETER READING			TOTAL MILES	
		From	To	Start	End	Distance (km)	Business	Private

Daily checks	Tires/ Wheel	Wipers	Lights	Mirrors	Horn	Seatbelts	Brakes	Coupling devices
Monday								
Tuesday								
Wednesday								
Thursday								
Friday								
Saturday								
Sunday								

Fuel Input					Notes :
Date	Quantity	Unit	Mileage	Units	
					Signature :

Vehicle Mileage Logbook

Sheet no.:

Make :   Model :   Year :   License number :

DATE	PURPOSE OF TRAVEL	JOURNEY		ODOMETER READING			TOTAL MILES	
		From	To	Start	End	Distance (km)	Business	Private

Daily checks	Tires/ Wheel	Wipers	Lights	Mirrors	Horn	Seatbelts	Brakes	Coupling devices
Monday								
Tuesday								
Wednesday								
Thursday								
Friday								
Saturday								
Sunday								

Fuel Input				
Date	Quantity	Unit	Mileage	Units

Notes :

____

____

____

____

____

____

Signature :

Vehicle Mileage Logbook

Sheet no.:

Make :   Model :   Year :   License number :

DATE	PURPOSE OF TRAVEL	JOURNEY		ODOMETER READING			TOTAL MILES	
		From	To	Start	End	Distance (km)	Business	Private

Daily checks	Tires/ Wheel	Wipers	Lights	Mirrors	Horn	Seatbelts	Brakes	Coupling devices
Monday								
Tuesday								
Wednesday								
Thursday								
Friday								
Saturday								
Sunday								

Fuel Input				
Date	Quantity	Unit	Mileage	Units

Notes :

____

____

____

____

____

____

____

Signature :

Vehicle Mileage Logbook

Sheet no.:

Make :   Model :   Year :   License number :

DATE	PURPOSE OF TRAVEL	JOURNEY		ODOMETER READING			TOTAL MILES	
		From	To	Start	End	Distance (km)	Business	Private

Daily checks	Tires/ Wheel	Wipers	Lights	Mirrors	Horn	Seatbelts	Brakes	Coupling devices
Monday								
Tuesday								
Wednesday								
Thursday								
Friday								
Saturday								
Sunday								

Fuel Input				
Date	Quantity	Unit	Mileage	Units

Notes :

Signature :

Vehicle Mileage Logbook

Sheet no.:

Make :   Model :   Year :   License number :

DATE	PURPOSE OF TRAVEL	JOURNEY		ODOMETER READING			TOTAL MILES	
		From	To	Start	End	Distance (km)	Business	Private

Daily checks	Tires/ Wheel	Wipers	Lights	Mirrors	Horn	Seatbelts	Brakes	Coupling devices
Monday								
Tuesday								
Wednesday								
Thursday								
Friday								
Saturday								
Sunday								

Fuel Input

Date	Quantity	Unit	Mileage	Units

Notes :

____

____

____

____

____

____

Signature :

Vehicle Mileage Logbook

Sheet no.:

Make : | Model : | Year : | License number :

DATE	PURPOSE OF TRAVEL	JOURNEY		ODOMETER READING			TOTAL MILES	
		From	To	Start	End	Distance (km)	Business	Private

Daily checks	Tires/ Wheel	Wipers	Lights	Mirrors	Horn	Seatbelts	Brakes	Coupling devices
Monday								
Tuesday								
Wednesday								
Thursday								
Friday								
Saturday								
Sunday								

Fuel Input				
Date	Quantity	Unit	Mileage	Units

Notes :

____

____

____

____

____

____

Signature :

Vehicle Mileage Logbook

Sheet no.:

Make : Model : Year : License number :

DATE	PURPOSE OF TRAVEL	JOURNEY		ODOMETER READING			TOTAL MILES	
		From	To	Start	End	Distance (km)	Business	Private

Daily checks	Tires/ Wheel	Wipers	Lights	Mirrors	Horn	Seatbelts	Brakes	Coupling devices
Monday								
Tuesday								
Wednesday								
Thursday								
Friday								
Saturday								
Sunday								

Fuel Input				
Date	Quantity	Unit	Mileage	Units

Notes :

Signature :

Vehicle Mileage Logbook

Sheet no.:

Make :   Model :   Year :   License number :

DATE	PURPOSE OF TRAVEL	JOURNEY		ODOMETER READING			TOTAL MILES	
		From	To	Start	End	Distance (km)	Business	Private

Daily checks	Tires/ Wheel	Wipers	Lights	Mirrors	Horn	Seatbelts	Brakes	Coupling devices
Monday								
Tuesday								
Wednesday								
Thursday								
Friday								
Saturday								
Sunday								

Fuel Input				
Date	Quantity	Unit	Mileage	Units

Notes :

____

____

____

____

____

____

____

Signature :

Vehicle Mileage Logbook

Sheet no.:

Make :	Model :	Year :	License number :

DATE	PURPOSE OF TRAVEL	JOURNEY		ODOMETER READING			TOTAL MILES	
		From	To	Start	End	Distance (km)	Business	Private

Daily checks	Tires/ Wheel	Wipers	Lights	Mirrors	Horn	Seatbelts	Brakes	Coupling devices
Monday								
Tuesday								
Wednesday								
Thursday								
Friday								
Saturday								
Sunday								

Fuel Input				
Date	Quantity	Unit	Mileage	Units

Notes :

____

____

____

____

____

____

Signature :

Vehicle Mileage Logbook

Sheet no.:

Make :   Model :   Year :   License number :

DATE	PURPOSE OF TRAVEL	JOURNEY		ODOMETER READING			TOTAL MILES	
		From	To	Start	End	Distance (km)	Business	Private

Daily checks	Tires/ Wheel	Wipers	Lights	Mirrors	Horn	Seatbelts	Brakes	Coupling devices
Monday								
Tuesday								
Wednesday								
Thursday								
Friday								
Saturday								
Sunday								

Fuel Input				
Date	Quantity	Unit	Mileage	Units

Notes :

____

____

____

____

____

____

Signature :

Vehicle Mileage Logbook

<table>
<tr><td colspan="8">Vehicle Mileage Logbook</td><td>Sheet no.:</td></tr>
<tr><td>Make :</td><td>Model :</td><td colspan="3">Year :</td><td colspan="4">License number :</td></tr>
</table>

DATE	PURPOSE OF TRAVEL	JOURNEY		ODOMETER READING			TOTAL MILES	
		From	To	Start	End	Distance (km)	Business	Private

Daily checks	Tires/ Wheel	Wipers	Lights	Mirrors	Horn	Seatbelts	Brakes	Coupling devices
Monday								
Tuesday								
Wednesday								
Thursday								
Friday								
Saturday								
Sunday								

Fuel Input					Notes :
Date	Quantity	Unit	Mileage	Units	
					Signature :

Vehicle Mileage Logbook

Sheet no.:

Make :   Model :   Year :   License number :

DATE	PURPOSE OF TRAVEL	JOURNEY		ODOMETER READING			TOTAL MILES	
		From	To	Start	End	Distance (km)	Business	Private

Daily checks	Tires/ Wheel	Wipers	Lights	Mirrors	Horn	Seatbelts	Brakes	Coupling devices
Monday								
Tuesday								
Wednesday								
Thursday								
Friday								
Saturday								
Sunday								

Fuel Input				
Date	Quantity	Unit	Mileage	Units

Notes :

____

____

____

____

____

____

Signature :

Vehicle Mileage Logbook

Sheet no.:

Make :   **Model :**   **Year :**   **License number :**

DATE	PURPOSE OF TRAVEL	JOURNEY		ODOMETER READING			TOTAL MILES	
		From	To	Start	End	Distance (km)	Business	Private

Daily checks	Tires/ Wheel	Wipers	Lights	Mirrors	Horn	Seatbelts	Brakes	Coupling devices
Monday								
Tuesday								
Wednesday								
Thursday								
Friday								
Saturday								
Sunday								

Fuel Input				
Date	Quantity	Unit	Mileage	Units

Notes :

____
____
____
____
____
____

Signature :

Vehicle Mileage Logbook

Sheet no.:

Make :   Model :   Year :   License number :

DATE	PURPOSE OF TRAVEL	JOURNEY		ODOMETER READING			TOTAL MILES	
		From	To	Start	End	Distance (km)	Business	Private

Daily checks	Tires/ Wheel	Wipers	Lights	Mirrors	Horn	Seatbelts	Brakes	Coupling devices
Monday								
Tuesday								
Wednesday								
Thursday								
Friday								
Saturday								
Sunday								

Fuel Input				
Date	Quantity	Unit	Mileage	Units

Notes :

____
____
____
____
____
____

Signature :

Vehicle Mileage Logbook

Sheet no.:

Make :   Model :   Year :   License number :

DATE	PURPOSE OF TRAVEL	JOURNEY		ODOMETER READING			TOTAL MILES	
		From	To	Start	End	Distance (km)	Business	Private

Daily checks	Tires/ Wheel	Wipers	Lights	Mirrors	Horn	Seatbelts	Brakes	Coupling devices
Monday								
Tuesday								
Wednesday								
Thursday								
Friday								
Saturday								
Sunday								

Fuel Input				
Date	Quantity	Unit	Mileage	Units

Notes :

Signature :

Vehicle Mileage Logbook

Sheet no.:

Make :   Model :   Year :   License number :

DATE	PURPOSE OF TRAVEL	JOURNEY		ODOMETER READING			TOTAL MILES	
		From	To	Start	End	Distance (km)	Business	Private

Daily checks	Tires/ Wheel	Wipers	Lights	Mirrors	Horn	Seatbelts	Brakes	Coupling devices
Monday								
Tuesday								
Wednesday								
Thursday								
Friday								
Saturday								
Sunday								

Fuel Input				
Date	Quantity	Unit	Mileage	Units

Notes :

____

____

____

____

____

____

Signature :

Vehicle Mileage Logbook

Sheet no.:

Make :   Model :   Year :   License number :

DATE	PURPOSE OF TRAVEL	JOURNEY		ODOMETER READING			TOTAL MILES	
		From	To	Start	End	Distance (km)	Business	Private

Daily checks	Tires/ Wheel	Wipers	Lights	Mirrors	Horn	Seatbelts	Brakes	Coupling devices
Monday								
Tuesday								
Wednesday								
Thursday								
Friday								
Saturday								
Sunday								

Fuel Input				
Date	Quantity	Unit	Mileage	Units

Notes :
____
____
____
____
____

Signature :

Vehicle Mileage Logbook

Sheet no.:

Make :   **Model :**   **Year :**   **License number :**

DATE	PURPOSE OF TRAVEL	JOURNEY		ODOMETER READING			TOTAL MILES	
		From	To	Start	End	Distance (km)	Business	Private

Daily checks	Tires/ Wheel	Wipers	Lights	Mirrors	Horn	Seatbelts	Brakes	Coupling devices
Monday								
Tuesday								
Wednesday								
Thursday								
Friday								
Saturday								
Sunday								

Fuel Input				
Date	Quantity	Unit	Mileage	Units

Notes :

____

____

____

____

____

____

Signature :

Vehicle Mileage Logbook

Sheet no.:

Make :   Model :   Year :   License number :

DATE	PURPOSE OF TRAVEL	JOURNEY		ODOMETER READING			TOTAL MILES	
		From	To	Start	End	Distance (km)	Business	Private

Daily checks	Tires/ Wheel	Wipers	Lights	Mirrors	Horn	Seatbelts	Brakes	Coupling devices
Monday								
Tuesday								
Wednesday								
Thursday								
Friday								
Saturday								
Sunday								

Fuel Input				
Date	Quantity	Unit	Mileage	Units

Notes :

Signature :

Vehicle Mileage Logbook

Sheet no.:

Make :   Model :   Year :   License number :

DATE	PURPOSE OF TRAVEL	JOURNEY		ODOMETER READING			TOTAL MILES	
		From	To	Start	End	Distance (km)	Business	Private

Daily checks	Tires/ Wheel	Wipers	Lights	Mirrors	Horn	Seatbelts	Brakes	Coupling devices
Monday								
Tuesday								
Wednesday								
Thursday								
Friday								
Saturday								
Sunday								

Fuel Input				
Date	Quantity	Unit	Mileage	Units

Notes :

Signature :

Vehicle Mileage Logbook

Sheet no.:

Make :   Model :   Year :   License number :

DATE	PURPOSE OF TRAVEL	JOURNEY		ODOMETER READING			TOTAL MILES	
		From	To	Start	End	Distance (km)	Business	Private

Daily checks	Tires/Wheel	Wipers	Lights	Mirrors	Horn	Seatbelts	Brakes	Coupling devices
Monday								
Tuesday								
Wednesday								
Thursday								
Friday								
Saturday								
Sunday								

Fuel Input				
Date	Quantity	Unit	Mileage	Units

Notes :

____

____

____

____

____

____

Signature :

Vehicle Mileage Logbook

Sheet no.:

Make :   **Model :**   **Year :**   **License number :**

DATE	PURPOSE OF TRAVEL	JOURNEY		ODOMETER READING			TOTAL MILES	
		From	To	Start	End	Distance (km)	Business	Private

Daily checks	Tires/ Wheel	Wipers	Lights	Mirrors	Horn	Seatbelts	Brakes	Coupling devices
Monday								
Tuesday								
Wednesday								
Thursday								
Friday								
Saturday								
Sunday								

Fuel Input				
Date	Quantity	Unit	Mileage	Units

Notes :

____

____

____

____

____

____

Signature :

Vehicle Mileage Logbook

Sheet no.:

Make :   Model :   Year :   License number :

DATE	PURPOSE OF TRAVEL	JOURNEY		ODOMETER READING			TOTAL MILES	
		From	To	Start	End	Distance (km)	Business	Private

Daily checks	Tires/ Wheel	Wipers	Lights	Mirrors	Horn	Seatbelts	Brakes	Coupling devices
Monday								
Tuesday								
Wednesday								
Thursday								
Friday								
Saturday								
Sunday								

Fuel Input				
Date	Quantity	Unit	Mileage	Units

Notes :

Signature :

Vehicle Mileage Logbook

Sheet no.:

Make :	Model :	Year :	License number :

DATE	PURPOSE OF TRAVEL	JOURNEY		ODOMETER READING			TOTAL MILES	
		From	To	Start	End	Distance (km)	Business	Private

Daily checks	Tires/ Wheel	Wipers	Lights	Mirrors	Horn	Seatbelts	Brakes	Coupling devices
Monday								
Tuesday								
Wednesday								
Thursday								
Friday								
Saturday								
Sunday								

Fuel Input				
Date	Quantity	Unit	Mileage	Units

Notes :

____

____

____

____

____

____

Signature :

Thank you!

WE ARE GLAD THAT YOU PURCHASED OUR BOOK!
PLEASE LET US KNOW HOW WE CAN IMPROVE IT!
YOUR FEEDBACK IS ESSENTIAL TO US.

Contact us at:

 log'Sin@gmail.com

---

JUST TITLE THE EMAIL 'CREATIVE' AND WE WILL

GIVE YOU SOME EXTRA SURPRISES!